Redemption Songs

KELLEY WOODEN-STANLEY

Redemption Songs
by Kelley Wooden-Stanley

Printed in the United States of America

ISBN: 978-0-9752921-7-4

Published by:
Gail Dudley, Highly Recommended Int'l
info.gaildudley@gmail.com

Cover Art by:
Dominiq Dudley
DominiqRDudley@gmail.com
1-929-265-2167

For my first super heroes:

My mother a Wonder-Woman
&
My Father a Super-Man

"We are going to emancipate ourselves from mental slavery because whilst others might free the body, none but ourselves can free the mind…"

—Marcus Garvey, Nova Scotia, October 1937

THANK YOU

First and foremost, I would like to thank my Lord and Savior Jesus Christ:

For there is no doubt in my mind from where my help, my strength, and joy comes from. A special thank you to Dr. Gene Harris and Dr. Charles E. Booth for their words of encouragement and understanding.

I would like to thank my family and my church family. Lastly, I want to thank my best friends

Angela, Tahita, Ricky(George), and my husband Kenny for loving me when I didn't love myself.

FOREWORD

To the committed Christian, redemption means to give up the bondage of sin for a new freedom in Christ, which is so beautiful that it is difficult to articulate, even for the most ardent believer. Dictionary.com defines redemption as the action of regaining or gaining possession of something in exchange for payment, or clearing a debt. Merriam Webster says that redemption is the act of making something better or more acceptance. At some point in our lives, we will find ourselves in need redemption. There will come a time when an action, word, deed, or perhaps even a thought, will necessitate restoration.

Kelley Wooden-Stanley helps the reader realize that redemption begins in the heart and soul and expands to the spiritual level. Through her storytelling and her prolific poetry, we learn that redemption is deeply personal and that one must first seek the liberation of her own soul before she can truly forgive another. After one particularly horrific attack, Stanley said, "My body hurt but my mind was safe." (p.15) She was on the road to redemption and forgiveness.

This work provides a voice for the thousands of women who have been savagely sexually assaulted, but suffer in silence because they are too ashamed to admit they have been victimized. It also speaks to families who ignore the signs of abuse or who do recognize the horror that has been perpetrated on a family member, but blame the victim instead of providing aid and comfort. She exposes why so many women remain silent about these assaults, "The biggest lesson I learned was to keep it a secret. I knew my community would blame me for the destruction of its mirage of being happy and wholesome." (p.16) Communities where women are objectified in exchange for the deification of men are called to account through the pain, suffering, and eventual emancipation that Stanley plainly reveals.

Undergirded by her strong and unwavering faith in Jesus Christ as her personal Lord and Savior, Stanley's autobiographical text shows us how forgiveness, healing, hope, love, and redemption can lead to a transformed life allowing those who have been broken to live devoid of guilt and shame. The reader will weep with her through the various tragedies, but find uplift and freedom in the beauty of her poetic prose.

This important work is a source for counselors and social workers whose mission is to usher in healing and hope to those whose sexual victimization, and other unforeseen circumstances of life, have left them in despair. It is a must read for those who want to rid the community of this scourge. Stanley's courage and determination has created a space for personal and community restoration.

Gene T. Harris, PhD, is a retired school district superintendent. She has degrees from the University of Notre Dame (BA, 1975), The Ohio State University (MA, 1979), and Ohio University (PhD, 1999). Her career in education spanned 38 years, retiring from Columbus (Ohio) City Schools in 2013.

ONE

The mind is an amazing thing, the dynamics of how it functions and works cannot be fully understood, or explained. When a person is in a car accident, the sudden flow of adrenaline, and how the mind will protect itself will not allow that person to remember the trauma, only a few details leading up to the accident. I wish this were true for victims of rape. One of the greatest crimes against a woman is the violation of her body in any form. It is a complete assault against the mind, body, and spirit. Long after the body heals the mind is still affected, and the soul suffers.

On a care free day, when I was 17, I went to the home of the guy who was my current boyfriend. The moment I stepped over the threshold of the door, the hairs on the back of my neck stood up, and deep inside I knew I should have left. Tragically, I stayed. As we watched television, he began to tug at my clothes, and began to fondle my body, making sexual advances to which I did not respond. I turned my nose up and asked him to stop as we were watching TV. He became more aggressive, and playfulness gave way to force. Loving kisses became harsh and rough. The tenderness that was usually present between us had vanished. I became nervous and wanted out. As I stood to leave he knocked me back down to the sofa, striking my lip. It instantly began to swell. He bent down and began to remove my blouse. My attempts to stop him were unsuccessful leading to a tug of war over my blouse. With a final jerk we were face to face. I begged and pleaded with him. My final question was "If you love me why are you doing this?" His response was "I would prefer you to hate me than to love me; that way I am always on your mind." I realized I was in for the fight of my life. I punched him and in response he shoved me to the floor.

I was in total shock. I was brought back to reality by the feel of the carpet under my hands while he dragged me toward the bedroom by my foot, as carpet burns blazed my back. I desperately attempted to find something to hold onto but my hands found nothing. When we reached his bedroom, I held onto the door frame and he began to unbutton my pants. I immediately released the door frame and attempted to stop him from reaching his goal. Crazed, high, and out of his mind, he was swift. Accomplishing the goal of removing my pants, he grabbed the center of my bra and immediately my body was raised off the floor as my straps began to cut deep into my flesh. Up on my feet, in shock, and realizing that I was losing I felt his hand grab my waist and in one instantaneous movement he shoved me to the bed. He pulled at my panties and they tightened and twisted from the powerfulness around my thigh. I felt my skin peel and give way as he forced them to my feet.

I continued to beg and plead. Not wanting to hear me, he covered my mouth with his hand and split my already swollen lips. The nightmare continued as he tried to enter my body, I attempted to keep my legs together. Focused and determined he used his knees to separate my legs. My thighs began to ache and throb then gave way; resistance was no longer possible. He entered my body with force and I immediately knew that I was bleeding. With each movement he made, pain radiated through my abdomen and down my legs. I closed my eyes and began to pray. I was transported to my childhood home, where I was sitting at the table with my family eating dinner. My body hurt, but my mind was safe.

As he finished, he stood to his feet and told me that I was dismissed. I grabbed my clothes, realizing that I was naked I knew I wouldn't make it to the car in the ice and snow. I ran to the bathroom and locked the door. As I look at my face in the mirror I barely recognized the reflection, but I told myself that Kelley was ok.

He wasn't finished. He began to bang on the door for me to open it. The more I refused the more he became angry. He began to kick the door, finally it gave way. As I coward against the wall he grab my hair, choked my neck and positioned my beaten body and entered me again, I didn't fight back. I told myself "Kelley just live, just make it home, just live, just make it home, just live…..Kelley, just make it home!" I do not remember leaving; I do not remember driving home. I became aware of my surrounding when the pain of attempting to undress caused havoc on my body. My shoulders, arms, back, thighs, legs, and face were battered, bruised, injured and very sore.

I awaken to the sound of my mother getting ready for work, and like every morning I knew she would peek in to tell me she was leaving I turned to the wall so that she could not see my face. (I continued this routine for days out of fear that she would know my shame). Hungry and needing water I slowly made my way downstairs feeling each step throughout my entire body. A pack of saltine crackers was on the table and I began to eat them, my lip began to sting and memories began to flood my mind and consume my thoughts. I was in disbelief. How could this happen to me twice?

At nine years of age early one afternoon I arrived at my friend's house. I knocked at the door and her older brother invited me in. I stepped over the entrance of the door and immediately the hairs on the back of my neck tingled. Being solely focused on seeing my friend I went further into the house and the door closed behind me. The memories of that day are vague, but the pain is clear. The sexual assault and hurt that I endured that day became a double edge sword in my life. One side showed me that I had to protect myself by learning what men wanted; the other side taught me to shield myself at all costs. The biggest lesson I learned was to keep it a secret. I knew early that my community would blame me for the destruction of its mirage of being happy and wholesome. I knew that my community was riddled with older individuals and even older traditions. At this time in society sexual assault was an accepted behavior from men, young and old. It would have been seen as my fault for being "fast." I knew that it would look bad for my parents. I knew that to protect my family and myself I had to keep quiet, and bear the brunt of what had happened.

Memories and pain, memories and pain then I became conscious of where I was and my current state. I sat in silence, alone with the lights dimmed crying and vowing I would never again be a victim. I swore to myself I would die before I let another person violate me. I shut down; I shut everyone out, I closed myself off from the rest of the world. I left a piece of me in that apartment on Innis Rd. the same way, pieces of a little girl were left at my friend's house: I was fractured. I was shattered but, I survived, I endured, I made it home, even though I was in pieces. My soul became quiet. My poetry stopped, my life became dark. My heart-beat stopped. I had ceased living. I learned that night that Kelley only had to survive.

Learning to live again would take me 20 years, one great church family and one very special man.....my husband, Kenneth.

PIECES

Heal me, O Lord, and I will be healed; save me and I will be
saved, for you are the one I praise
—Jeremiah 17:14

Raped, battered, and bruised
Who gave him the right to abuse?
He took from me
Something that was divine
To think about that day
Nearly blows my mind.

He beat me down
Till I was dang near broken
Couldn't tell anyone
They would think I was joking.

I was his punching bag
How could anyone not see?
The terrible things he had done to me.
I was freight
What a horrible sight
He created that night

My swollen eye
My lip he split
He bruised my thigh
I cried to the Lord
And asked him why.
As he choked my neck I thought
I would die

My spark that once blazed oh so bright
Was almost snuffed out
That very night.
I became broken pieces
I was coming undone
Who could have known?
I never told anyone
The shame I felt
The sorrow I bore
Became much more.
Despair won out
The Kelley I knew
She was fading out.

God whispered and said
Hold on to me true.
The things that I've done for others
I can do for you to.
He wrapped me in HIS arms
wiped away my tears
Then tended to my wounds
Until they were healed.

Look at me now
Head held high
Not one tear do I cry
For that awful night
When one man's plight
Was to destroy my light
That shined so bright

Here I stand
On my own two feet
Proving to the world
I could not be beat
That one man's shallow mind
Enraged and so blind
Could not define
My destiny in time
All praises I give
To God up above
He healed my broken pieces
And made me
Feel loved.

Two

In April 2009 I awoke to excruciating abdominal pain. At that time it was the worst pain I had ever experienced. I was totally debilitated. I was unable to get our little one ready for her day and I was unable to prepare myself for work. The worst part was that I had to wait for my husband to return home to aid me in the simplest of tasks. This morning would be the first of many visits to the emergency room. After many months of being pain free suddenly in August 2009 I returned to the emergency room with the same complaint and with the same pain. I was admitted to the hospital for further testing. In December of 2009 I was diagnosed with Crohn's disease. I was devastated, as I knew there was no cure. My only hope was prayer and treatment.

The ER trips continued. Along with me on this journey, that included periods of being well and periods of being sick, was my husband. Through every hospital admission, every test, and every night of pain management he was there. I happened to wake from a sleep that was induced from Morphine one night. I looked over and noticed Kenny sleeping again in an uncomfortable chair. As I stared at him, I began to notice my heart beat. I actually drifted back to sleep staring at him and listening to the beat of my own heart. A sound I had not noticed since 1989. It was there that my love and passion for poetry reclaimed my heart. I believe that it is not by chance that my love for my husband was infused with my love for poetry. This infusion would change my world forever.

HEART BEAT

For this reason a man will leave his father and mother and
be united with his wife, and the two shall become one flesh.
—Ephesians 5:31

When my heart beats,
My heart beats double.
One for me
for you the other.

When my heart beats,
My heart beats strong
Constantly thinking,
Praying
Longing for
No other.

When my heart beats
It counts each second
As each beat passes
It waits for the next one.

When my heart beats,
It beats with you in mind
Never forgetting the love
that binds.

When my heart beats,
It beats focused
and true
Knowing the love
we have will last
till it's thru
When my heart beat..........

THREE

ഝ

hen my parents separated, I was suddenly thrown into a world that was new and strange. My life changed from a house to an apartment, from familiar to unfamiliar, from money to little money, from a family unit to a broken family, from a close bond with my father to phone calls, and visits. Everything was new. Little did I know that it began a passage in my life that would include the greatest lessons that I would ever learn. One lesson that began early was the discernment of good and bad friendships.

Across the hall from our apartment lived a girl and her family who I befriended. We became close; we became best friend and confidants. We were kindred spirits with our passion for rap groups like Whodini, and RunDMC. We hung out, and we stayed very busy. As my family began to rebound from its changes, and my bond with my father reestablished, her father was sentenced to prison. We found support in one another. We grew and changed but our friendship stayed. I thought this friendship was unshakable. Years later my friend became pregnant and managed to keep it from her mother for many months, but it was revealed to me in the strictest of confidence. I felt it was my duty as a friend to stand beside her and encourage her in every way possible. She was my best friend and I loved her like a sister. Life for her changed with a child; mine changed with marriage even though neither she nor I was prepared for the roles of mother or wife. Suddenly thrown into an adult world, with adult situations, and adult responsibilities, our friendship showed cracks of separation. When my husband and I moved to a new city my friendship with her was on life support and as the years pressed on, it eventually died.

When my husband and I were preparing for our 20th wedding anniversary, I longed for one thing. I wanted to rekindle the friendship that I thought had isolated us from many dangers, seen and unseen, during our teen years. I reached out to her many times. Each attempt returned with emotionless responses. She made it clear that this friendship was cancelled with no hope of ever being resurrected. In her final email she stated…….."Some people come into our lives for a lifetime, a season, or a reason, please stop all communication with me." I knew she was absolutely correct. It hurt my heart; I felt abandoned. I wanted to cry. This hurt me to my core being, shook my soul, and took my breath away. After all the years that had passed, I still considered her a best friend.

I realized that my three other closest friends, Tahita, Angela, and George were honest, deeply rooted friends and they were the ones who gave meaning to steadfast, unwavering, and immovable friendship. We are all still connected and I love them to this day. I hold them near and dear. They were patient, kind and understanding. They loved me when

I didn't love myself. For them I would lay down my life. It is with them in mind that I dedicate the poem, "To Dance."

Upon the final moments of reading her email I prayed for her, wishing her nothing but a life of happiness and success. I miss her and will cherish our years as friends. God bless her where ever she may be. .

TO DANCE,

As iron sharpens iron, so one man sharpens another.
—Proverbs 27:17

You turned your back
You walked away
You said the sun had set
And now you were done.

You said our friendship
Was only for a season
Couldn't last any longer
It had no reason.

You said a lot
I heard every word
As much as I tried
Your heart was cold.

Just couldn't believe it
Was I hearing you right?
It cut me so hard
It cut like a knife.

Hard to hear
My heart did hurt
That pain in my chest
From A Friendship lost

The bond was broken
The tie unbound
I'm missing a friend
My God what now?

But wait hold on
A voice to me said….

I am mighty and great
In all things I do
What is one friend?
She was lucky to have you.

The sun I will raise
And set just for you
The next rainbow you see
It's because of my promise to you

Don't cry for one friend you are so loved
From me here in Heaven
And others that you love.

Look over there I see your Mom and Dad
Isn't that Dear?
Gleaming and smiling
With not one tear to be had

I see you received
The gifts that I gave
Your sisters and brother
Your friends and husband
Kamille, Kameron and Kamya too
That house on the corner designed just for you.

Some friends do come for just one season but never
Forget that I am the reason
I give you the rain
I give you the sun
I wake you every morning
With the touch of my finger
And I nudge from my thumb.

So never fear
You're never alone
One friend couldn't handle
The blessing I've done.

You lost one friend
And I gave you much more
Too many to name,
too much love
to measure
What is one friend?
When you have much better.
I will never leave you
Forsake nor abandon
The things that she said
I know you can handle

Dance in the sun
Dance in the rain
Dance in the snow
Dance away the pain.
How special you are
I see the light within
That's where you will find me
Your constant friend

FOUR

I was blessed to have been born into a family that was absolutely great. My parents had six children: Patricia, Kathy Jo, Kristina, Karl, Karen and me: Kelley. My grandmother, who also resided with us, was affectionately called Dear. Holding down the household was my father, Joseph and my mother, Marion. My mother was always about business; she took no foolishness. Spoke quietly, demanded the best from us, was graceful and elegant but ruled like a quiet storm, comforting yet powerful.

My favorite holiday has always been Thanksgiving. Every year Thanksgiving revives the memories that are deep within me, as my home fills with familiar smells of years long ago. I recall many times running downstairs on Thanksgiving Day morning to watch the parade on television, only to be greeted by a kitchen that was full of food, and a buzzing house that was full of excitement and love. My mother's talent for cooking is still unmatched. My mother and our kitchen were the beating heart of our house. Her cooking was intertwined with love, fellowship, and lessons.

A few lessons learned from my mother came not from her presence, but from her quick and untimely departure from this life. Momma taught me that life is a vapor, and constantly fleeting. She taught me to hold onto moments because life changes minute by minute, and although roses smell wonderful when they are alive, when they die we are able to have potpourri.

In what would be our final moments she gave me understanding, honesty, and clarity. These were the things I had searched for my entire life. With her final words to me she taught me what it would take to be a "Momma." Her last request of me was to pray with her. I delayed her all day as my walk with Christ was new, and I was nervous to pray in front of her. It was the first time our roles were reversed, it was the first time she wasn't praying for me but I was praying for her. I was afraid. I wanted the Lord to hear me. I wanted him to heal her. Then I realized what I wanted most for her was comfort and peace. I wanted her to be pain free. For the first time I was unselfish. When I could no longer give her excuses I held her hands and opened my heart and prayed with my mother. Those were the last words she ever heard me say. I still love and miss her, a rose that has become potpourri…still giving.

A ROSE

For my momma
Marion L. Wooden
October 12, 1935-December 23, 1993

If I could:
I would give my mom a rose
I would give her my eyes to see its deep red petals
Hands to feel it velvet softness
Nose to smell its sweet fragrance...
Mouth to taste the cool air that surrounds it
Ears to hear the whispers of its beauty
If I could I would give my mom one more day
To give my mom a rose.

Honor your father and your mother,
so that you may live long in the land
the Lord your God is giving you.
—Exodus 20:12

FIVE

During one of my hospital admissions I was beginning to wear thin. I was tired of being a patient, tired of the atmosphere, tired of feeling useless. I longed to go home, not just my place of residence but my real home. The city I was born in Columbus, Ohio. I missed family, friends, the laughing and joking, the every day good feel of being around people I loved and that loved me. I was beginning to feel down. As I looked around my room I began to wonder when I was going to be able to return home and there was a knock on my hospital door. In walked a man I had never seen before. He introduced himself as Chaplain Cory.

I was delighted. I had a visitor. He was interesting, very well groomed and educated. We began to talk, and I remember thinking God had sent a friend my way. How right I was. Chaplain Cory and I talked as if we had known each other for years, it was as though time had once again stood still and we shared a few moments as friends. In the midst of our conversation, Chaplain Cory asked me "how you deal with everything?" I was confused because no one had ever asked me that. I didn't have an answer because I did not know myself. I was faced with the hard reality that I was just surviving from one medical flare up to the next. Then I remembered…..poetry. I told him that I write poetry. He asked me to read a little bit if I had it. I opened my laptop and began to read. As I watched him intensely, I noticed he closed his eyes and I realized he could visualize what I had written, and although we were in my hospital room, my words had transported us to the same place. Upon finishing I began to speak of another poem that I was writing, but I was stuck on its progression. Chaplain Cory encouraged me to push through the writing block that I had, he encouraged me to continue writing, and stay committed in the blessing God has bestowed upon me. I knew from that day, that Chaplain Cory was a person I would never forget. I knew our friendship had just begun.

Since our initial meeting, our friendship has grown; he has continued to give me advice, and words of encouragement, as well as opportunities to share my gift. Through our relationship, we have met the other's spouse and connected on a spiritual level that could only be explained and summarized by the fact that there is no doubt God was the orchestrator in our friendship. I love Chaplin Cory and I celebrate that God placed him in my life , another blessing

My poem "Power to the People" is with Chaplin Cory in mind. From the moment he stepped into my hospital room, he has encouraged, supported, politely pushed, advised, reassured, cheered and applauded me. He walks boldly and excitingly in the light of Christ. Chaplain Cory is a great friend and I appreciate him. God has empowered all of us to aid and help others. Chaplin Cory gives true meaning to "Power to the People."

POWER TO THE PEOPLE

For God did not give us a spirit of timidity, but a spirit of
power, of love, and of a self-discipline.
—II Timothy 1:7

The quest for freedom, justice and equality
Is bigger than the world we see
It shatters the hope of the Constitution
It surpasses the expectation of
the Emancipation Proclamation
With its ups and down
Twist and turns
It is laced with sadness,
and intertwined with love,
and yet and still
Power to the people

Hands up, Don't shoot
Just might
Save a few.
Help me!
I can't breathe
Are words that
went unheard.
Stand your ground
Is still around
Killing our youth
Without remorse
How many to count

Have been choked out.
How many lives
Have been cut short
Handle by police
some breath
No more.
How much more
Can we endure?
And Yet and still
Power to the People

Separate but equal
Separated people
white hoods, capes and gowns
no strange fruit
hanging around.
Stop and Frisk
Can't hail a cab
Driving while black
You may end up dead
Methods used to catch
Runaway slaves
Can still be seen this very day
And Yet and still
Power to the people.

Brutalized, lynched, tarred
And feathered
Ask African Americans
Have things gotten better.

A bag of skittles
A can of tea
People dying senselessly.
Scottsboro boys
Central Park 5, Jena 6
All black lives,
Innocent until proven guilty
Not that I see
And yet and still
Power to the People

Pay is low, debt is high
People doing everything
      To get by
Babies sick, dying in the womb
Kids that are here
Face life with gloom
Poor education
No one's up for the task
Everything requires a bill to pass
No books, no art, no music to be
Learned.
Prisons are better equipped
With video games, emails
And cell phones.
Who can afford a doctor to see
Parents are struggling to feed
Their families
And yet and still
Power to the People

How many lies
Does it take
To cover up
Some people
Mistakes
He had a weapon
He was threatening me
He fit the description
He was trying to flee
What must be done?
To set us free
From the inequality
Of justice we see.
How can this be
turned around
black kids are dying
In every town.
And yet and still
Power to the People

Power to the Blacks , the Whites
The Yellow and Red
Power to the young.
Power to the old
Power to the bold
Power to fight
Power to heal
Power to do God's will
Power to love
Power to Share
Power to show someone you care

Power to stand
Power to shout
    "Hatred won't take us out"
Power to you
Power to me
Power to everyone
    We see.
Power to Justice,
Freedom and Equality
And yet and still
Power to the People.

Six

Teachers are bestowed the influence to cultivate and build children up as well as tear them down. With this power, they hold places in hearts and lives forever as individuals from all over the world recall what teachers have taught them through the years. For me, my past is riddled with excellent teachers, but as with so many instances there were a few bad ones. In fourth grade I was not the best student nor was I the worst. I longed to learn but found myself shy and a follower. I wore many faces to fit in where the authentic me would not have. One day for reasons which escape me, I was held in for recess yet again. I was the only one. Alone, angry, and upset I felt as though again this teacher had picked me out to berate. As recess was ending and I stood by the door to join my class at the restroom, my teacher came nose to nose with me and informed me that "I would never amount to anything." I felt as though my soul had been struck down, and my throat went dry. My knees began to shake and I felt fearful, but of what I had no idea. Even now I can see her bee-hive hair-do, her cat glasses, her expression, and every wrinkle on her face. I became bitter and bitterness resonated in every aspect of my life. That is the day I had ceased learning in her class and school became a chore. This incident which I never spoke of lived with me until the day that I entered the halls of East High School.

East High School rich in tradition, and bursting with "tiger pride" was the right place for me! This would become my home away from home, with what would become "family." Teachers like Mr. Georgeff, Mrs. Raduege, and Mr. & Mrs. Brown took an interest in all. It was their mission to instill in us more than just book knowledge. They took teaching personally; they made loving us a life mission; they protected us as though we were their own; and we students loved them in return. They insisted on teaching us to value ourselves regardless of skin color, family problems, family status, or history. We were valued as though we had been born in the White House!! They never allowed us to believe that we were second class citizens, or that we were three-fifths of any human. I remember these teachers and many others with fondness. I did not comprehend at the time the calling these individuals accepted. These teachers were Caucasians, teaching in a predominantly black school at a time when unity among the different races was low. These teachers, along with numerous African American teachers from East High School, were unified in their mission to ensure we were educated and ready for life's challenges and opportunities. These teachers are modern day heroes. They are the ones who refused to allow students to stand on an auction block and be sold to a life of crime, alcohol and drugs, or to be devalued as a person.

Three-Fifths

My command is this: Love each other as I loved you.
—John 15:12

This country was designed
With not me in mind
Do you see me?
Do you see who I am?
With my chocolate brown skin
Like I was molded in God's hand.

According to the Constitution
I am three-fifths of what you see.
And this is the land of the free?
This is the home of the brave?
Took a civil war for us to be saved

My ancestors came here
Snatched from their homes
Chained to a boat
Cold and alone
Some made it here
Some met the sea
Countless of them died
From sickness and disease.

Stood on a block
Hands roamed free
Sizing them up
Examined every cavity

There was no privacy
No secrets,
No rights,
Slave owners were
Buying African lives
Outright.

Massa made his visits
By cover of night
Increasing his slave population
With his very own
And yet
They called Africans
Savages, barbaric, and uncivilized
Who back then was telling lies?

Picked cotton
Till their fingers cracked
and bled
Broke their backs
Survived on scraps
Lived in shacks
All this from the land of liberty
Not from what I see.

Sung their songs
While working in the fields
Letting runners know when the
Coast was clear
Escaped at night
By the full moon light

Led by a star
That guided them far
Making an exodus
To a better place
Where freedom wasn't bound
By anyone's race.

Many reached the north
Some were returned
How many others were tied, hung and burned.
One nation under God
Who should be shamed?
Who's been using whose name in vain?

Attempting to re-write history
Cleaning up the things we know
Renaming the middle passage
Making it all just for show
Forgetting those Africans
That stood on the block
And watched in horror
Their lives ripped apart.

Never paid a salary
Not one penny or dime
And we're supposed to
Forget all this in time.
A debt is owed
This country can never pay
For bringing those Africans over
in those awful chains

Is justice for all
Or just for a few
Seems like that Lady
Can pick and choose
Reparations aren't charity
Gauged by the things
That I've learned
Reparations are what
My ancestors earned.

SEVEN

For my two girls I have always wanted them to know that they were beautiful, no matter how they looked or what they wore. I always wanted them to know that beauty comes from inside, it comes from deep within and reflects outward, that beauty is in the eye of the beholder and they should be beautiful in their own eyes regardless of the world's opinion.

My mother was a hairdresser by trade, but never practiced her trade outside of our home. Every Saturday we would line up. We would have our hair washed, and later sit still for her to press and curl our hair. Hair was never an issue for my mother. She would often say "cut your hair and it will grow back." This view transcended into her views of just who we were as her children. She allowed us to express who we were, as long as it was respectful and it was tasteful.

My sister Karen is 7 years older than me, and to this day we express ourselves differently but over the years we have found out that we actually have the same taste. My sister is all business; she is straight laced, very stylish, and always the professional. My sister's profession centers in an office. I am the complete opposite. I love tennis shoes, would live in jeans (if I could), and built a career working in a laboratory. Karen s hair is straight, I wear locs, but we chose to style our hair the same way. Karen lives in a ranch style house, I chose a colonial, but both houses have red front doors. Karens' voice is very distinguishable, and office friendly. I am a spoken word artist. We are truly ying and yang, two versions of beauty, two versions of style and grace.

During the difficult years when my sister and I had sisterly squabbles, my mother recognized our differences, and never took sides. She saw the beauty in both of us. She cultivated it by allowing us to be ourselves. I would reach adulthood before I valued our differences and accepted our similarities. It was years after our mother passed that our relationship would be cemented, and cherished. I cannot imagine my life without her.

Momma taught us that black is beautiful no matter if it is in dress shoes or tennis shoes, and that beauty is everything in the reflection that we see. Whether we are looking at each other or looking in a mirror, beauty is what we see.

MIRROR

Your beauty should not come from outward adornment,
such as braided hair and the wearing of gold jewelry and
fine clothes. Instead, it should be that of your inner self,
the unfading beauty of a gentle and quiet spirit,
which is of great worth in God's sight.
—I Peter 3:3-4

Black is what I see.
I look in the mirror
And black looks back at me

From the crown of my head
To the soles of my feet
... From my deep dark eyes
To my voluptuous size
Black is the color that speaks.

My kinky hair
With my thick luscious lips
The cross of nose
With my spacious full hips
As I gaze in the mirror
What is it that I seek?
But all I hear is black
Whispering to me

My breasts are large
My ass ain't flat
My stomach is round
As I look around

Black gazes back.

Black speaks so softly
That I couldn't hear
Than all of a sudden
I hear it so clear
Black is speaking to me
In my ear

Look beyond the mirror and
What do you see?

You are beautiful and great
You are one of a kind
That mole on your back
Is God's design
Created and crafted
And baked by the sun
Every ripple and curve is
Where God put his thumb

Never question your beauty
Just by what you see
Black is only a color
Its only skin deep

Those kissable lips
Your dark lovely eyes
All of your curves
And those soft chocolate thighs
Your hair is different
It's very unique
What man couldn't value
The reflection I see.

I looked in the mirror
And what did I see.
Beauty personified looking back at me.

EIGHT

Summer time is always thrilling for children. School is out, and the fun begins. Vacation bible school (VBS) was always held during these care free months. A week of learning Bible lessons and at the end of the week there was always a program that children participated in to show everyone just what they had learned.

During one of these weeks I did not know that VBS teachers gathered names of the individuals who were not members of the church. At the end of the program, people were asked to stand if your name was called. Several names were called including mine, as I never became a member of the church I was raised in but I was the only one to stand.

As I stood to me feet the Reverend began to speak as though I was an errant child, and began to me inform me of the ramifications of me choosing not to be baptized. The more he pressed me to join, the more I refused, the more defiant my spirit became. Finally in disgust with the fact that I still refused he began to tell me that I was going to hell that I would not see my mother, father and family who would be in Heaven, and I would burn forever in hell. He said to me that I was choosing the devil, and making him happy, that I was causing God to cry because I refuse to turn myself over. I stood there shaking, knees buckling, and nauseated. I wanted desperately to sit down, to fade into existence. I wanted no part of this church that was full of fire and brimstone. The tactic had just the opposite effect; it drove a wedge, and built a resistance that would last for years. I began to cry and my defiance for church took root.

After what seems like an eternity of being demoralized, embarrassed, and ostracized my teacher grabbed my hand, and told me to sit down as she boldly spoke claiming I was just a baby. She became a focus point for me as she stared me in the eyes. She explained to me that when I was ready I would know, and how that was between me and Jesus. I was in a church full of people and yet felt alone, I felt as though God had abandoned me. I longed for my parents' presence but they too were absent that evening. I never attended Vacation Bible School again and continue to struggle with the closeness of Sunday school.

Words can build a nation, or cause one to crumble. Words can hurt, harm and kill. The power of words is evident throughout time, but never has it been more evident than at the beginning of time. The world came into existence by the power of words. Words have the power to bring someone closer to Christ or drive them farther apart. Words should always be chosen carefully.

Spoken Words

In the beginning God created the heavens and the earth.
—Genesis 1:1

The word was first
The word was
The word is
The word shall always be
God spoke the words
Let there be
Then it began
The tick of time
Heaven was formed
Earth was born.

Light once bound
To dark
Twisted, turn, then
Spun apart
Light became day
Dark became night
God spoke the words
Day one had come and it was done

A blue vault raised high
God spoke sky
Beauty twirled and swirled
Became embraced
By the clouds that took shape
What a sight to behold
A vision so bold

Dry land appeared
God named it earth
Got its own space
Water gathered
In one place
So vast, so big
God spoke seas
It came to be.
All things green
Created a scene
Plants and trees
All bore seed
God said produce
Fruits and herbs
All from words

The sun
The moon
God decorated the sky
Two great lights
Bright One for day
Dimmed One for night

Hung the twinkling stars
For a perfect sight
Days, weeks, years
All seasons began
Right here

Day five every bird
Flew high
Fish swam with ease
In the water of the seas
God said
Be fruitful and increase
No matter the size
Large or small
God created them all

Let there be:
God spoke the words
For every
Creeping, crawling, walking beast
From dinosaurs to a lions roar
From elephants sounds
To the tiniest ants
On the ground.
Everything began to roam
Under the vaulted dome.

With dust in hand
God made man
From the image of three
God spoke the words

Blew air in mans lungs
His heart
Began to beat
With power over all
Creation not yet complete
God put Adam fast asleep.

A rib from Adam
Eve was created
Hard on the outside
Soft in the center
Bone of bone
Flesh of flesh
United as one
God spoke the words
First marriage was blessed
All of God's creation
At its best.
Six days had passed
On the seventh God rested.
The word was first
The word was
The word is
God spoke the word that's how everything came to be.

NINE

When my sister Kathy was pregnant on one occasion she travelled home and spent the night. I awoke to find her in the sitting room. As I descended down the steps she called my name. Excited I was happy to see her. We sat and chatted. The sun was beaming in the window; it was quiet, and very serene. It was picture perfect. As we sat and shared this moment, she placed my hand on her belly. I felt my niece kick and move. I was in awe. Every time I would place my hand in a different spot, she would kick. I was certain my niece knew I was present. This would begin a life long love and a close bond with my niece that many could not understand, but a bond that would last through the toughest of times. We have been close from the beginning. My sister Kathy recognized and knew from where Karlotta and my relationship began.

Kathy's family nickname was Katherine the Great. Although it began out of fun, she deserved the title. Kathy was good at everything. She was bright, smart, and intelligent. Kathy also suffered from the disease of being bi-polar. Kathy had the highest of highs, but also suffered some pretty terrible lows. She was also unfortunate to have suffered with this disorder before it was well known, or understood. Kathy's great escape from reality, suffering and her past came in the form of drugs and alcohol.

In writing the poem "Journey", I replayed Kathy's life in my head from the end to the beginning searching for what went wrong. I searched for answers. I searched for an opportunity to know Kathy better. One incident, one night, one crime, one travesty stood out in my mind. The night Kathy was raped by a "cousin". That night Kathy was out past curfew and when my parents arrived home our father and mother noticed that Kathy was just returning home. A confrontation between my father and Kathy ensued, and escalated. That night I witnessed Kathy receiving a beating that left her body battered and bruised and left me confused and afraid. My father called her a whore not thinking of it ramifications. Kathy and my father were never the same. Early the next morning we realized Kathy had left. No one ever took the time to hear her story, or her agony. I never had the courage to tell her that we shared a common story of survival. I often wonder if we had shared our experiences with one another would it have helped ease our pain. It saddens me because I will never know.

Although the poem "Journey" is not her life, nor is it mine, it was not hard to understand the struggles of drug addicts. As I looked around, I began to remember the stories that I had heard over the years from other individuals that had shared their own darkness with me. The poem "Journey" became and ode to compassion for the sufferers of drug addiction.

August 2003 the life of my sister Kathy ended here on earth. My world lost a shining star. My world became smaller. My world changed. I lost a sister. Kathy's journey had come to an end, but she left me a great gift. She left me my niece Karlotta.

JOURNEY

In him we were also chosen, having been predestined
according to the plan of Him who works out everything in
conformity with the purpose of His will.
—Ephesians 1:11.

Am I human
No more
Because my
Journey
Is different from
Yours.

Never told anyone
I was molested
At four
Watched my mom
Turn tricks on
the kitchen floor.
Turned 13 my
Time came around
Mom took the money
Smelly men laid
Me down

Starving hungry
No food to be found
Went to sleep
Many nights
With a grumbling sound

School became
A problem
As I struggled
To read
Couldn't tell a
D from a B
An F from an L
My 3's looked like E's
Labeled a dummy
I couldn't spell.

Teachers couldn't
Take the way
That I smelled
My urine soaked clothes
My filthy hair
Had lice three times,
Gonorrhea twice.

Am I human
No more
Because my journey
Is different from
Yours
Put heroin
In my veins
To release all pain.

As a child my
Dreams was not
To become a
Cheat or a whore
I had BIG dreams
Of becoming more.

My favorite belt
Tighten around
My arm
As beads of sweat
Begin to form

Mouth starts to
Water as I strike
The match
To cook the dope
My body lacks

Needle goes in
Finds a good spot
Relief floods over me
My head begins to nod.

Heroin is strong
It packs a mighty punch
One day on top
Of the world
Next day in a slump

Euphoric and bliss
Floating on a cloud
My mind goes blank
My body starts
To shake
Then falls to the ground

Bold bright light
Shining in my face
Why am I strapped
Down in this strange
Familiar place

My doctor walked over
As I hid my face
You've been here before
he glanced
At me and said
If you don't get help
You're going to wind up dead

Oh Lord Jesus
Please help me
I am a sinner
Yearning to be free.

Am I human
No more
Because my Journey
Is different from yours.

I look to the heavens
And begin to pray
Release me Lord
I don't want to
Die this way

God spoke to me
In a quite low voice
I am that I am
I knew you before you were formed
I see all your pain
But I love you so much more
Go in peace
You can beat this disease
I gave you everything
You will ever need.
Take comfort and know
Your debt for sin
Has been paid with
3 nails
1 cross
The world was never
The same.

Trust and believe
I am with you all your days
When you're feeling lonely
I am a prayer away

30 days clean
I begin to feel ok.
60 days went by in a blink of an eye.
90 days gone
My life takes shape
One year later,
College life is great.
Five years down, as I don my
Cap and gown
Am I my brothers' keeper?
yes I am
Passed all my tests.
I am a counselor now.

I owe it all to Him
The Lord most high
My heart still beats
I am still
Alive!

TEN

I was inspired to write the poem "The Jeffersons" when I returned home one weekend. It was just my little one and me. As I drove down a popular street, I could remember who lived where and events that may have occurred in the past. It broke my heart to see the houses in disrepair and dilapidated. A community once busy so full of life practically lay desolate. What a tragic turn of events. Then I realized that everyone had moved out, everyone had moved on, everyone including me!

In 1968 the Fair Housing Act was signed by President Johnson. This single act made it possible for this transition of housing possible. We as a people as African Americans were now able to live in areas that were once considered "exclusive." Although I am grateful for the opportunity, I think of the ones who seem to not have been able to "get out" either by circumstance or choice. It can make one feel like we have left soldiers on the battle fields to fight the wars in these communities-- wars of education, wars of drugs and criminal activity, wars of murder and prostitution, wars to save neighborhoods from collapse, wars to redefine these once great neighborhoods.

THE JEFFERSONS

Live in harmony with one another.
Do not be proud, but be willing to associate with people
of low position. Do not be conceited.
—Roman 12:16

Are we moving out?
Because we're moving up
Leaving our neighborhoods
Desolate and stuck

Was it crack?
That did them in
Or the breakdown of families
Where only moms are putting time in
Dads are missing
And can't be found
God only knows when they
Will come around

What happen to the neighbors?
That always kept watch
Being our neighborhood crime cops.
Vacant signs are what we see
As bricks of memories lay at our feet.
Liquor stores are everywhere
Spreading poison anywhere
Kids look for love from somewhere
But they're being led nowhere.
Corrupt politics are so profound

Elderly lives are spiraling down
Bad healthcare
No doctors to see
Who in the hell don't want to flee.

Are we moving out?
Because where moving up
Leaving kids and babies
Running out of luck
Murders and robberies
Are the things we see?
Watching in amazement
Like it's on TV.

Men are killed
Left bleeding in the streets
Prostitution is
Some ladies defeat.
How much more can
Young ones contend
When the lives they lives
Comes to a quick end.
Eulogies are written everyday
Dreams of degrees
Fade away.

What once was thriving
And full of pride
Reduced to rumble
Then multiplied

Divided by drugs
Add some grief
That brings the summation
Of the things we see.

Are we moving out?
Because we're moving up
With violence and killing occurring everyday
Who in their right mind would want to stay?

ELEVEN

After marrying my husband I would eventually attend the church where he had been a member for his entire life. I was there, physically, but I had failed for years to turn my life over to Christ. I had failed to join church, failed to step out on faith, I failed to believe Christ loved me. As the third year began I had a private conversation with the pastor of the church…. Dr. Charles E. Booth. I bore my inner most secrets, I showed him my shame, I exposed my soul, I removed my protective shield and allowed him into my innermost being. In return I received nothing but love and understanding. Above all I received acceptance. I did not realize at the time that he would become a great influence and fill numerous gaps that were left open by the departure of many in my life. Pastor Booth whom, I love dearly, has a great sounding voice and when preaching one has only the resolve to listen. He is a remarkable teacher. When I began to write the poem "Son Kissed," it was his voice that resonated with me. I could hear the roll and thunder of his deep voice saying "Ahh…Kelley now you're on to something!" or I could hear him saying "No Kelley, that doesn't go there," as though he was beside me. I would hear his voice coaching me unto the end of what I thought to be one of the most important poems I was to write. "Son Kissed" is the story of Jesus Christ life from birth to resurrection, and I had to get it right. Who better to coach me through this difficult poem than a man I admire, who better than a man anointed to preach God's Word. My Pastor, Dr. Charles E. Booth, holds a special place in my heart. There are not enough words in all the languages combined to express how I am grateful that God saw fit to place him in my life.

Son Kissed

For God so loved the world, that he gave his only begotten
Son, that whosoever believeth in him shall not perish
but have everlasting life.
—John 3:16

My heart has been kissed
By the Son
Enamored, captivated and
in love with the Holy One.

Birthed in a manger
Wrapped in swaddling clothes
Didn't have a place
To call his own
Secretly Herod called
Wise men three
To find the
Young One born to be King.

They looked to the sky
Where a star shined down
It led them to a place
Where Christ could be found.

The wise men
Fell upon their knees
To worship the little one
Sent from above
Gave three gifts
To God's only
Begotten Son.

Throughout His
Lifetime we all
Should be amazed
At the things He did
And the people He saved.

With two fish and
Five Loaves
He fed a few thousand
The power He showed
In saying a blessing.

His light so bright
He gave the blind their sight.
Spoke sound into the ears
That could not hear.

Twelve years a woman bled.
Held down by a plague
Yet she still believed
One day she'd be freed
With a touch of his hem,
Christ looked at her and said by your faith
You are healed.

Met an unclean spirit
Who acknowledged Him
Legion was their name
He sent them packing
No longer could they stay
That demon was extracted.

With all power
In his hand
He calmed a raging sea
Then walked on water
As if land was
Beneath his feet

Given a choice they favored Barabbas
Curcify crucify crucify Him
The crowd shouted
King of Jews
They all doubted

Beat him all night long
Gave him a crown of thorns
Soldiers mocked and spat
On him
And struck Him
In the head
All the while not one
Word He said

Stretched His arms wide
nailed Him to a cross
pierced his side
Christ spoke to the Father
And then he died
The skies grew dark
The clouds began to cry
My Lord
My Savior
They crucified.

Three days later ......

The world began to shake
Death was no place
For one so great
An angel appeared
Claiming the one you seek
Is not eternally asleep
He is not here
Rolled the stone back
It became so clear

Jesus defied them all
Birthed from a virgin womb
He had no need
For a borrowed tomb
His place is with the Father
Not somewhere dark with gloom

Alive and well In Galilee
with holes in His hands
And holes in His feet
Christ…A risen savior for you and for me.

I am who I am
Because
God is
and
Jesus did
So I can't help but to forgive……

ABOUT THE AUTHOR

Kelley Wooden-Stanley is the youngest of six children born to late Joseph and Marion Wooden of Columbus Ohio. She attended and graduated from East High School in 1989 where she met her current husband of 27 years. Kenneth and Kelley have three beautiful children, and four grandchildren. She began to further her education at Columbus State Community College then later would attend Capella University with a projected completion date in fall of 2018 with a Bachelor's Degree in public safety specializing in Criminal Justice. Kelley and her family moved to Cincinnati Ohio in 1996 and is currently employed at Cincinnati Children's Hospital. With a fervent desire to reside closer to family and reunite with Mt. Olivet Baptist Church her immediate family returned to Columbus Ohio in 2016. Her love of writing poetry ceased for over twenty years from personal turmoil and tragedy, but would later resurface and result into a stronger and spiritual level of writing.

To book Kelley to speak for your event contact by email:

kelleywrites123@gmail.com

To order additional books contact
Kelley Wooden-Stanley at:

kelleywrites123@gmail.com

REFLECTIONS

_____

_____

_____

_____

_____

_____

_____

_____

_____

_____

_____

_____

_____

_____

_____

_____

_____

_____

_____

www.ingramcontent.com/pod-product-compliance
Lightning Source LLC
LaVergne TN
LVHW091226080426
835509LV00009B/1194